MW00886446

Greek

Mythology

©Copyright 2017 by Cascade Publishing

All rights reserved.

It is not legal to reproduce, duplicate, or transmit any part of this document in either electronic means or in printed format. Recording of this publication is strictly prohibited.

CONTENTS

Heroes

Aside from featuring gods, Titans, and magical beasts, the Greek mythology is also replete with numerous heroes with awe-inspiring stories. Most of them have immense strength, agility, and intelligence. Compared to those of an average mortal, their skills and intellect are way more superior because of their unique parentage. Usually, one of their parents has been a god or goddess, giving them superhuman traits.

Some of the most popular examples are Heracles (son of Zeus) and Daedalus (son of Athena). In some cases, however, even a mortal with a normal parentage can also become a hero. A great example of this one is Jason, a prince from Iolcus. Under Chiron's tutelage, he managed to obtain the wisdom and strength to lead the Argonauts in the quest for the Golden Fleece.

In this chapter, you will discover more about the greatest heroes (as well as the uncommon ones) on Greek mythology. In this chapter, you will learn more about the amazing feats of the Greek heroes.

Jason

Jason was a Greek hero who came from a royal bloodline. Sadly, he was not able to enjoy the benefits of being a king because his uncle, Pelias, took the throne for himself.

Pelias threw Jason's father in prison and he planned to murder him when he was still a baby. Thankfully, his mother managed to sneak him out of the castle and send him to Chiron, the most intelligent centaur in Greece. The creature took great care of Jason and taught him the essential skills he needed for survival, such as hunting, plant lore, and even civilized arts.

When the young hero grew up, he embarked on a long journey to reclaim the throne that was stolen from him.

In the sacred halls of Mount Olympus, the gods were cooking up an elaborate plan for Jason to test his skill and mettle as a hero. While the mortal was travelling back to his hometown, Hera sent down a violent torrent.

He was waiting for the storm to pass when he saw a wrinkly old woman approach him. She asked Jason if he can carry her just across the stream.

The young hero did not even think twice in helping the old lady. He carried her towards the other end of the stream, despite the violent water currents. He staggered, but he continued bravely on his journey. While he was crossing the river, one of his sandals was swept away by the current, making it hard for him to find his bearings on the soft ground.

An Oracle once told King Pelias that he should watch out for someone who is wearing a single sandal. This means that Jason was really destined to remove his uncle from the throne.

The old lady that he carried to the other side of the river was actually Hera. Even today, the stories are still unclear whether the goddess revealed her true form to Jason or if she just helped him on his journey without revealing her true identity.

After a long trip, Jason finally arrived in his hometown. He claimed that the throne is rightfully his, but his uncle was too stubborn to give up. To add to his list of problems, King Pelias was not aware that the person in front of him was Jason, the nephew that he planned to kill a long time ago.

The king questioned Jason's capability of ruling the entire land, so what he did was he gave the hero an interesting challenge. While they were eating, Pelias started a conversation with Jason. He asked the hero to suggest a way to get rid of a person who is giving you a lot of problems. Jason suggested sending that person on a quest to look for the Golden Fleece. King Pelias was happy with the idea, and told the hero to embark on that specific quest.

Naturally, the hero accepted this mission. But before he started, he first searched for companions who can help him out. Even though searching for the fleece was deemed an impossible quest, it was not too difficult for Jason to find a crew. In fact, there was even a surplus of other heroes who applied for the position. The chosen heroes who joined Jason were called the Argonauts. Some of the characters who joined were Heracles and Atlanta, a strong-willed heroine.

Jason and his crew rode on a ship that was constructed by Argus, one of the most celebrated shipwrights in Greek mythology.

On top of Mount Olympus, Hera was overseeing the progress of Jason's journey. She collaborated with Athena, the goddess of wisdom and crafts. She visited the heroes and gave them a prow that is made from timber found in Zeus' sacred grove. The magical properties imbued in the prow allowed it to speak and tell prophecies using a human voice.

The adventures of Jason and the Argonauts were not easy. On the eve of their journey, they reached an island populated by powerful women. The inhabitants despised the Argonauts, so they had to fight fiercely just to get out of the island.

Another adventure that they had was with King Phineus. This unfortunate leader once offended the god, and since then, he has been plagued by the Harpies. These were creatures that have a woman's head, the body of a bird, razor sharp claws, and horrible table manners. Whenever King Phineus is having dinner, the Harpies would swoop down on his table to create a loud racket. In addition, they would also defecate on his meals. Anyone haunted by these horrible creatures during mealtimes will surely lose their appetite. Because of this situation, the King became thin and weak.

Thankfully, some of the Argonauts were relatives of the North Wind. Their unique lineage allowed them to fly. Using their powers, they chased the Harpies away, and the King was able to eat his meals in peace from then on.

To thank the Argonauts, the King taught the crew how to get past the Clashing Rocks, or the Symplegades. He even taught them useful techniques in making a mechanism that can prevent their ship from getting damaged. Thanks to King Peleus, Jason and his crew remained unscathed throughout the entire trip.

After getting past the Clashing Rocks, the crew managed to reach Colchis, the place where the ram with the Golden Fleece lived. This particular ram once saved a man from being sacrificed to the gods. To thank the deities for saving his life, Phrixus offered the ram and gave the fleece to Colchis so they can hang it in a grove.

However, catching the ram was not their biggest problem. The largest hurdle that they need to face was the ruler of the barbaric place, King Aeetes. This king hated visitors because most of them attempted to steal the fleece. Instead of showing the Argonauts hospitality, the King asked them to go away. However, Jason and his crew were persistent and demanded Aeetes to hand over the fleece.

Even though King Pheneus hated his visitors, he wasn't able to punish them because his daughter, Medea, intervened. She hasn't met these people before, but the princess was willing to help them out because Aphrodite made her fall in love with Jason.

It was easy for the goddess to make the lady fall head over heels with the Greek hero, considering that she was the goddess of love. This burning infatuation became the key for the Argonauts to steal the fleece. Medea managed to talk to her father, so instead of punishing Jason and his crew, the king asked them to complete a task.

King Phineus commanded the crew to plow his field and reap the harvests of his farm, all in one day. If they managed to do that, the king will give them the fleece. The task seemed easy, but the challenge here is the two fire-breathing bulls guarding the field. These creatures do not have an ordinary body. Instead of flesh, their bodies are made of brass. Their horns are so sharp that they can rip a man in half.

Medea, who was secretly a master of the magical arts and potion-making, gave Jason a special salve that can make him immune to the Colchian bulls' flames. After he tamed these creatures, he used them to plow the field.

Then, Jason planted the special seeds that King Phineus gave earlier. Little did he know that these seeds were actually a set of dragon teeth. Once they were planted on the ground, they blossomed into fully-armored, huge, and muscular warriors. They attacked Jason, but the hero was already briefed by Medea about this. She told Jason that he needed to throw a rock at one of the warriors. They're not that smart, so the seed warrior hit by the stone will think that one of his teammates did it. This made them lose their focus on the heroes and fought each other to the death. When the day ended, Jason and his crew defeated the seed warriors without even lifting their swords.

After the warriors were defeated, it was time for Jason to get the fleece. Medea led him to a large tree that was protected by an even larger dragon. In the middle of the tree was the Golden Fleece.

Jason was about to attack, but the love-struck Medea advised him to hold his weapon first. Then, she took out a sleeping potion and then sprayed it on the dragon. While the monster was sleeping, they crept forwards to steal the fleece.

When Jason finally got the item he was looking for, he abandoned Medea and sailed back to his hometown. Jason promised the woman that he will love her forever, but he found another princess upon returning home and married her instead. This broke Medea's heart, and she brought her misery with her to the grave.

Odysseus

Similar to Jason, Odysseus is not a demigod (half-God and half-human). However, he became one of the most memorable characters in Greek mythology due to his charm and intelligence. In fact, he was one of Athena's most favorite mortals.

Odysseus played a central role during the Trojan War because he was the one who came up with the idea of hiding inside a giant horse. However, Homer also gave him his own story and named it The Odyssey. This one tells his decade-long journey to Ithaca, and the events that happened after the Trojan War.

Odysseus was considered as one of the smartest heroes in Greek mythology and he was a great leader who served as an inspiration to his fellow warriors. Furthermore, he was also well-known for his unwavering devotion to his family.

Homer's tale began right after the fall of Troy. Due to their victory, the Greeks became boastful and disregarded the gods. As punishment, the gods destroyed their ships and killed most of the warriors. Odysseus got caught in these attacks even though he was one of the few warriors who did not forget to thank the gods for giving them victory.

The Greek hero drifted towards Ogygia, the island where Calypso was living in solitude. The kind enchantress nursed Odysseus back to good health. Calypso longed for a companion, so she detained the hero for several years. By that time, most of the other Greek heroes who survived the Trojan War safely returned to their hometown, and it was only Odysseus who has yet to complete his journey home. The enchantress Calypso thought that by using her beauty and promising him the gift of immortality, she could make the hero forget about Penelope, his beloved wife. However, his love for his wife and child never faltered.

Thankfully, the gods showed compassion towards Odysseus and decided to help him return home.

Meanwhile, Athena visited his son, Telemachus, and asked him to embark on a journey to find his father. The boy travelled from Pylos to Sparta, and he even met Menelaus and his wife, Helen. The king showed the boy hospitality and told him about his father's adventures.

In the island of Ogygia, Zeus and his son Hermes asked the enchantress to free Odysseus from captivity. She begrudgingly complied, but she made sure that the hero was well-prepared for his journey.

While the hero was traversing the seas, Poseidon created a powerful storm and destroyed his raft. He was then saved by a minor sea goddess and helped him drift safely to the island of the Praeacians. They welcomed him with open arms and showed him hospitality. In return, Odysseus told them about his epic adventures.

His tale began after the fall of Troy. Odysseus and his men were heading home to Ithaca. However, they first visited the island of the Circones and raided their city to grab some provisions.

Next, they visited the island of the lotus-eaters. The inhabitants of this place got their name from eating the sweet fruit of a special lotus plant. This particular fruit was like a drug; once you eat it, you will lose all your desire to leave the place.

Several of Odysseus' men ate the fruit, so he literally dragged them back to the ship and tied them tightly just so they could sail peacefully.

Their next adventure was in the land of the Cyclops. These creatures are one-eyed giants who have a savage and brute nature. Polyphemus, one of the Cyclopses, managed to trap the heroes in a cave by blocking the only entrance with a huge boulder.

Then, the savage giant picked off the crew and ate them one by one. Most of the survivors lost hope, but Odysseus did not give up and created a plan to escape.

By observing Polyphemus, the hero discovered that the giant was very protective of his sheep. The Cyclops kept his flock inside the cave, and he only brings them outside during feeding time. In order to escape Polyphemus, the crew must impair the creature's vision and blend in with the flock.

One day, Odysseus sneaked behind the Cyclops and stabbed his eye using a wooden stick. While the creature was shrieking in pain, they hid themselves among the flock and escaped.

Once they got out of the cave, they ran towards their ship and sailed immediately. Polyphemus threw rocks in their direction, but they easily dodged these.

Afterwards, the crew arrived in the dwelling place of Aeolous, a minor god whose responsibility was to keep the winds in check. Aeolus was quite happy with Odysseus' visit, especially when the hero recounted all their tales. Because of this, the minor god gave them a bag filled with storm winds. Using this gift, the crew will be able to reach Ithaca in no time at all. Unfortunately, one of his crew members became too curious with the bag of winds. He opened the pouch, thinking that it contained gold. Strong gusts of wind blew forth and the entire crew was tossed back to the land of Aeulous. Sadly, the god refused to help them for the second time and requested that they leave immediately.

The crew sailed once more until they reached the isle of the Laestrygonians. Similar to the Cyclops, these creatures were also huge, powerful, and savage. The monsters destroyed most of Odysseus' ships and ate his men.

After barely escaping the Laestrygonians, they finally reached the isle of Circe, another powerful and cunning enchantress. Circe cast a curse on Odysseus' crew and turned them into small pigs. The hero was not affected by the spell because Hermes gave him a magic herb. Since Odysseus was the only one who was not turned into a pig, he managed to force the enchantress to reverse the spell. When his men returned to their human form, Circe welcomed them as honorable guests and threw them a feast.

Odysseus and his crew stayed there for almost a year. The enchantress advised that they visit the underworld and seek the guidance of Tiresias, a blind Greek who has the power to give prophecies. Even though they were a little bit hesitant, they still pushed forth and went to the land of the dead.

Tiresias gave Odysseus a lot of useful pieces of advice to help him reach Ithaca safely. In addition, he also told the hero about the dangers that he'll face once he returns to his hometown, as well as how he can escape them. Aside from the blind prophet, he also met familiar spirits such as Achilles, other Greek heroes in the Trojan War, and Anticlea, his mother.

After visiting the underworld, the crew returned to Circe's island. The enchantress gave him some advice about the other potential dangers that he'll be facing while sailing home. This included the Sirens – maleficent sea nymphs that lure unwary sailors using their captivating melodies.

Out of curiosity, Odysseus requested his crew to tie him up on the ship's mast so that he could listen to the siren's song without putting himself in danger. The rest of the members wore ear plugs so they could still control the ship while passing the sirens.

In addition, they also encountered other monsters such as Scylla and Charybdis. These large creatures guarded the narrow channel where the ship needed to pass through.

After barely surviving the wrath of Scylla and Charybdis, they reached the land of Helios. This place was filled with sheep and cattle that were sacred to the gods. The blind prophet and the enchantress warned Odysseus that these animals should not be harmed. Unfortunately, some of his crew did not heed this warning.

When they set sail again, Zeus created a huge storm that destroyed their remaining ship. The rest of Odysseus' men drowned during the storm. The Greek hero drifted alone until he reached Calypso's island, where his story all began.

After hearing Odysseus' exciting but sad stories, the Phaeacians took pity on the hero and offered to give him a ship so he can return to Ithaca. No more storms had crossed his path because Poseidon was finally willing to put aside his anger and allowed Odysseus to return home.

Athena appeared to the Greek hero when he reached Ithaca. The goddess told him that Penelope was plagued with a lot of suitors who were rude and evil. However, she assured Odysseus that his wife remained loyal to him throughout the years.

The hero did not reveal his true identity when he reached his homeland. Instead, he dressed up as a beggar and stayed in a swineherd's home.

Athena fetched Telemachus, who was still in Sparta. When the boy met his father, they crafted a plan to fend off Penelope's suitors.

The next day, Odysseus returned to his palace while still wearing his beggar's clothes. Most of the suitors mocked him as he walked past the halls. Penelope wasn't aware that it was Odysseus. Thankfully, she decided to talk to the beggar. She told him that for several years, she has been working on a shroud for Laertes, Odysseus' father. She told the suitors that she refuses to marry until she finishes this shroud. She managed to make the weaving process last for years because she would weave the cloth in the morning and then unravel it at night. Sadly, this trick was discovered and her suitors were forcing her to finish the shroud immediately.

While she was busy talking with Odysseus, a nurse went inside the room and offered to wash the beggar's feet. The nurse recognized the scar on his leg, so she managed to discover his true identity. However, Odysseus ordered the nurse to keep the secret to herself.

The next day, Penelope presented a challenge to her suitors. She took out a bow and arrow that belonged to her husband. She told her suitors that whoever manages to pull the bow's string and shoot the apples lined on one side of the room will be her husband. All of the suitors failed the task.

Then, Telemachus requested that the beggar be allowed to pull the string. Since the weapon was the property of Odysseus, it was easy for him to wield it. After accomplishing the task, he revealed his true identity. Together with Telemachus, he killed all of the suitors.

After his struggles ended, Odysseus lived a long and happy life with his family.

Heracles

When you were a kid, you probably learned about this hero from the popular Disney film *Hercules* (which was also the Roman version of his name).

While the animated movie managed to capture his heroism and immense strength, a lot of details about Heracles' life were left out.

One of these was his attitude. Heracles can sometimes be very rash and hot-tempered. But he was also very simple and straightforward.

Just like the other Greek heroes, Heracles was also a demigod. His father, Zeus, fell in love with a mortal lady name Alcmene. This woman was already married to Amphitryton, but Zeus still impregnated Alcmene while her husband was away. Hera discovered Zeus' infidelity and tried to prevent the baby from being born.

Alcmene still gave birth, and she named the baby Heracles. In Greek, his name means "Hera's precious gift." This made the goddess even angrier, considering that she never really wanted this child to be born.

Afterwards, Hera sent two large snakes upon the baby's crib. However, Heracles inherited his father's immense strength. With his small hands, he strangled the snakes and killed them before they could bite him.

Hera knew that she won't stand a chance of fighting head-to-head with Heracles or Zeus. So in order to get back at her cheating husband, she decided to make the rest of Heracles' life as miserable as she can.

Over the years, Heracles grew up to be a powerful warrior. He had a wife name Megara, and he also had two healthy children. For a while, the family lived a very happy life. However, it did not last for long, because Hera started to unveil her plan for revenge.

One day, the goddess cursed Heracles with a fit of madness. A murderous rage came over the Greek hero and he killed his wife and children using his bare hands.

When Heracles finally came to his senses, he begged the god Apollo to purify him again. Apollo said that in order to clean his spirit, he needed to do several tasks. These came to be known as the 12 labors of Heracles.

In addition, Apollo also ordered the hero to visit the land of the Tiryans. This kingdom was ruled by Eurystheus, which proved to be a big problem for Heracles because the king was known to be mean and tough. The hero must serve the king for 12 years, but the good news is that by completing the task, his soul will be purified and he can even gain immortality.

Heracles' struggles were the greatest embodiments of **pathos**, a Greek idea that pertains to achieving fame and glory after overcoming the biggest struggles in one's life.

The first impossible task that Heracles faced was the Nemean Lion. King Eurystheus asked the hero to bring the skin of the lion that was terrorizing Nemea. This creature is extremely feared because its fur was invulnerable to any weapon.

Heracles tracked the lion in a cave underneath the Nemean hills. It had two entrances, so he blocked off one of them so that the lion cannot easily escape. Since no weapon can pierce the lion's thick hide, Heracles used his large, muscular arms to choke the monster to death.

The king was amazed at Heracles' superb strength. However, Eurystheus also started to fear the hero. After the first task, the king banned Heracles from entering the city. In addition, he also created a buried pathway in the ground just in case he needed to escape from Heracles.

Eurystheus also started giving his commands to Heracles via a herald, and he refused to meet up with him ever again.

The next task was to kill the Lernean Hydra. As its name implied, this creature would rise from the deep swamp of Lerna and ravage the countryside. This serpent had nine heads that spew poison. The beast also had a huge body and one of its heads was immortal.

Accompanying him on this quest was Iolaus, his nephew. Iolaus had already joined Heracles in his previous quests, and he was known for his skills in riding the chariot.

The battle between Heracles and the Hydra was fierce. First, he shot the creature with a volley of burning arrows. When the beast emerged from its hiding place, Heracles tried to seize it with one of his hands. The Hydra in turn wound its coils around his foot so that it will be harder for him to escape. Using a large club, Heracles smashed the Hydra's head. But every time he crushed one of the creature's heads, two more would pop up in its place.

To kill the monster, Heracles asked Iolaus to burn the headless tendons of the hydra's head so that the replacement heads won't grow in its place. When the eight heads were destroyed, Heracles chopped off the immortal one. Afterwards, he buried it underneath the ground.

The King was not too impressed with the hero's feat. Eurystheus said that this labor did not count because Iolaus helped him.

For the third labor, Heracles needed to capture the hind of Ceryneia.

Ceryneia was a small town located fifty miles from the kingdom of Eurystheus. The hind, meanwhile, was a female red deer.

This third task seemed a little bit easier compared to the first two. However, Heracles faced several challenges while capturing the hind. First, this creature had bronze hooves and golden horns that can be used for attacking its captors. In addition, it was Diana's (goddess of the moon) favorite pet. As such, Heracles was not allowed to neither kill nor capture this sacred beast. Hera was already angry at him, so he couldn't risk incurring the wrath of another goddess.

Heracles chased the deer for more than a year. When the creature grew tired of the chase, it rested under the mountain called Artemisius and then attempted to cross the Ladon river. But before the hind can cross, Heracles shot her with an arrow.

Diana and Apollo appeared before the hero while he was on his way back to Mycenae. Of course, the goddess was mad at Heracles for injuring her most precious pet. She would've punished him, but the hero told the truth instead. Heracles told Diana that he was only doing this because he was obeying what the oracle said. Afterwards,

Diana calmed down and tended to the deer's wound. He brought the deer to Mycenae, but the goddess took it back after Heracles presented it to the king.

For his next task, Eurystheus commanded Heracles to capture the Erymanthian boar alive. Similar to the other creatures, this pig is huge, wild, and had an extremely bad temper. It was named the Erymanthian boar because it dwelled on the mountain of Erymanthus. The creature would ravage the nearby village every day, leaving behind dozens of injured men and animals. While tracking the beast, Heracles first visited a cave where his centaur friend, Pholus, was living. The hero was hungry and thirsty, and the centaur was more than willing to give him sustenance.

When Heracles had his fill, he proceeded to hunt the boar. Inside the cave where it dwells, the hero can hear the creature snoring. When the boar woke up, Heracles chased it around the mountainside.

When the beast ran out of breath, it hid in a huge thicket. However, its hiding place was not large enough to cover its body completely. Heracles poked his spear into the creature's hiding place and he drove it towards a field covered in snow.

Afterwards, the hero trapped the pig using a net and then hauled it back to Mycenae.

The fifth labor was about cleaning the Augean Stables. The challenge here is that Heracles needed to clean the stables in just one day.

King Augeas, the owner of the stables, boasted of having the largest number of livestock in Greece. His farm bred bulls, goats, horses, and a whole lot more.

Heracles visited the King and told him that he's willing to clean his stables, provided that he would give him a tenth of his cattle herd. The King could not believe his luck. The stables have not been cleaned for several years, so you can just imagine how filthy it was.

In addition, it was also a dangerous place because the horses were carnivorous and had sharp teeth that can tear through human flesh.

For this task, Heracles created a huge opening on the wall near the cattle yard. Afterwards, he punched another hole on the other side.

Then, he went to the nearby rivers and dug a trench. He connected the stream of the two rivers so that it will flow through the stables and flush out the mess on the other side of the hole.

After cleaning the stables, the king discovered that Eurystheus was the mastermind behind all this. As such, he decided not to pay Heracles.

And since the hero was not able to get the cattle herd, the King of Mycenae decided that the fifth labor did not count.

For the sixth labor, King Eurystheus ordered the legendary hero to fend off the flock of birds that gathered near Stymphalos. In some versions of the story, the Stymphalian birds were man-eating creatures and they were as fierce as lions or leopards.

The lake where the birds gathered was located deep in the middle of the woods. Heracles did not have any idea how to drive those creatures away from the city. Thankfully, the goddess of wisdom helped him out with this task. She gave him a pair of bronze krotalas, which are instruments similar to castanets and which created loud clapping sounds. The krotalas were created by Hephaestus, the smith god, so these were imbued with unique properties.

Heracles climbed on top of a mountain. Afterwards, he clapped the krotala. The loud noise was enough to scare the birds away. Afterwards, Heracles shot a volley of arrows at the flock of birds and killed them on the spot.

After fending off the Stymphalian birds, Heracles went to Crete to dispose of the Cretan Bull. The current ruler of the land was King Minos, a very powerful leader who had great control over the several nearby islands.

Crete was the home of most bull stories in Greek Mythology. It was also in this kingdom where Zeus transformed into a large bull and took Europa away from King Minos. In addition, the Cretans were also fond of the bull-leaping sport wherein participants will grab the horns of the beast and hold on to it for as long as they can.

The particular bull that Heracles needed to face was a gift from Poseidon. The Cretans promised that they would sacrifice this creature to the sea god. However, King Minos deemed that the bull was too beautiful, so they sacrificed a different one instead. Poseidon was furious with this, so he made the bull go mad and attacked the villagers. Minos' wife, Pasiphae, fell in love with the creature, and she gave birth to the Minotaur. This creature had the head of a bull and a body of a man. The king locked up this monster inside a labyrinth underneath his kingdom.

Heracles easily disposed of the Cretan bull that was ravaging the city. He brought it to King Eurystheus, and he allowed the creature to roam free. It wandered around Greece, leaving destruction in its path.

Theseus was the one who killed the Cretan bull when he visited the city of Marathon. Afterwards, this hero went to the Labyrinth and killed the Minotaur.

Heracles' eighth labor was to steal the man-eating horses of Diomedes, the ruler of the Bistones tribe. The challenge here is that these savage creatures must be alive when he delivers them to King Eurystheus.

This time, Heracles was accompanied by a band of strong volunteers. They easily beat the grooms who were taking care of the creatures. They were about to steal the horses from their stables when suddenly, the soldiers of Diomedes emerged to recapture the animals. Heracles entrusted the horses to a young man named Abderos so he could join the fight.

Abderos was weaker than Heracles, so the mares dragged him around the road until he died. After killing Diomedes and his soldiers, Heracles went back to Mycenae and gave the horses to the King.

His next task was retrieving Hippolyte's belt. The task was a little bit difficult because the owner was the queen of the Amazons, the strongest tribe of female warriors. This tribe lived separately from the men. They would only take the female ones whenever they gave birth. During childhood, their new tribe members would be trained to become strong warriors.

Hippolyte's belt was given to her by Ares because she was the strongest warrior among the Amazons. This accessory is used for carrying her spear and sword. King Eurystheus wanted this belt so he can give it as a present to his daughter.

Heracles' friends were worried about him. He was facing a whole army by himself, so his chances of survival were very slim. That's why his friends decided to accompany him again on this very dangerous mission.

It took them a long time before they finally reached the land of the Amazons. While Heracles and his crew were settling the ship in the harbor, Hippolyte came to visit them.

She asked why the men visited the island, so Heracles told her the truth. The queen was willing to give the belt without the need to spill blood. However, Hera assumed that the arrival of these men on the Amazon Island meant huge trouble. To fix the problem, the goddess disguised herself as one of the warriors and spread rumors that Heracles will take their queen.

Of course, the Amazon army flew into a rage and attacked the ship. Heracles saw the women approaching from afar and he knew that they were under attack.

Then, he unsheathed his sword, killed Hippolyte on the spot, and took her belt. Instead of running away, Heracles and his crew fought the rest of the Amazon warriors.

The tenth labor was supposed to be Heracles' last one. But since the king did not count two of his other tasks, he needed to accomplish two additional labors.

For the tenth task, the Greek hero must take a trip to the farthest corner of the world and steal cattle from Geryon, son of the Chyraor and Callirhoe. Geryon was a creature with three heads and three pairs of legs connected to a single waist. He got this unique shape due to his special family lineage. His father, Chrysaor, sprang forth from the Medusa's body after Perseus chopped off her head. Callirrhoe, meanwhile, was Oceanus and Tethy's daughter.

Geryon lived in Erythia, a mountain found between the borders of Europe and Libya (During the ancient times, the borders of Europe were considered as the edge of the world.). Orthus guarded Geryon's herd of red cattle. This hound-like creature was the brother of Cerberus. However, he only has two heads instead of three. The red cattle were herded by the hero Eurytion.

On his journey to Erythia, Heracles fought a lot of monsters. In addition, he also created two huge mountains to commemorate this labor. When the hero arrived in Erythia, Orthus suddenly attacked him. Heracles was quicker so he easily evaded the attack. Then, he smashed the hound with his club. Eurytion attacked next, and he met the same fate as his beloved dog.

While he was running away with the cattle, Geryon chased them down. Heracles fought fiercely, and he killed the monster by shooting it with arrows.

Stealing the cattle herd was easier compared to the actual journey of bringing them back to Mycenae. The two sons of Poseidon tried to steal the bulls while Heracles was travelling to Liguria. They fought fiercely, but he managed to kill them both.

When they reached Rhegium, one of the bulls escaped and swam to the sea. It reached Sicily and then crossed the neighboring country. It was then captured by the King Eryx, one of Poseidon's sons.

To capture the bull, Heracles temporarily entrusted the rest of the herd to Hephaestus. The hero found the cattle in Eryx' herd and he asked the king if he can have it back. Of course, Eryx refused and challenged him to a wrestling match. Heracles was not the type of hero who would back down in a fight. He managed to beat the king three times in wrestling until he finally killed him. Afterwards, he took the bull and returned to the rest of the herd.

After months of travelling, Heracles finally reached the Ionian Sea. However, Hera was still determined to prevent the hero from finishing his quest. The goddess sent down a swarm of gadflies to attack the herd of cattle. The entire herd scattered far and wide, forcing Heracles to run around Thrace. The hero blamed his misfortune on the river Strymon. So what he did was he filled it with rocks so that it would be impossible for other people to traverse the river.

After gathering the herd of cattle, he brought them to Eurystheus, who in turn sacrificed them to Hera.

Eight years have passed since Heracles completed his first labor. However, the king of Mycenae still demanded two more tasks from him. So for his eleventh labor, Eurystheus demanded Heracles to give him the apples of the Hesperides. Hera gave this apple tree to Zeus as a wedding gift. This meant that it would be impossible for the Greek hero to complete this task without utterly getting thwarted by the goddess.

In addition, the apple tree was guarded by Ladon, a hundred-headed dragon, and the Hesperides, powerful nymphs who were daughters of Atlas.

One of Heracles' major problems was that he doesn't know where to find the apple tree of the Hesperides. He travelled to Libya, Egypt, and even Asia just to find the tree. Along the way, he embarked on several adventures. Kyknos, the son of Ares, challenged him to a fight. When their duel was interrupted by a huge thunderbolt, Heracles journeyed further to Illyria. He found Nereus, and Heracles commanded the sea-god to tell him the location of the sacred apple tree. Before Nereus told him the answer, he transformed into different kinds of monstrosities just to escape Heracles' strong, iron-like grip. However, the hero did not waver and held on to him. After some time, the sea god became frustrated and just told him the location of the apple tree.

While travelling to the northern edge of the world, Heracles was stopped by Anteus, another son of Poseidon, who challenged him to a wrestling match. Heracles was more than willing to oblige, and he defeated Anteus immediately. Since Anteus drew power from the ground, Heracles lifted him up and crushed him in midair.

Then, he was captured by Busiris, Anteus' half brother, Heracles was about to be used as a human sacrifice, but he escaped and killed Busiris.

He also met Prometheus, the Titan who gave man the gift of fire. The hero was travelling to Mount Caucasus when he saw the Titan bound in chains. Every day, an eagle would swoop down and eat his liver. As an immortal Titan, Prometheus' liver would grow back, and he had to endure the eagle's wrath again. This torture would have continued until the end of time, but Heracles came to his rescue. He killed the eagle and freed the Titan from his chains.

To thank the Greek hero for freeing him from his bonds, Prometheus told him a vital secret in getting the apples. In order to kill the dragon and fetch the apples, Heracles needed to free Atlas, the Titan who was carrying the earth and sky on his shoulders.

To convince Atlas to kill the dragon, Heracles must temporarily carry the weight of the sky while the Titan was doing his job.

After Atlas successfully retrieved the apples, he told Heracles that he'll deliver the fruits to King Eurstheus. This seemed like an act of generosity, but the Titan's real intention was to leave Heracles behind and carry the sky for the rest of his life. The hero agreed, but he first asked Atlas if he could lift the sky for a little bit so he can put some padding on his shoulders.

The Titan put the apples down and switched places with the hero. Heracles picked up the bushel of apples and delivered them to Eurystheus. Atlas' plan to escape his punishment was thwarted thanks to the hero's quick thinking.

Sadly, Eurystheus was not allowed to have the apples forever since they belonged to the gods. After all the pain that Heracles went through just to get these fruits, Athena took them back and returned them to the northern part of the world.

The final and most dangerous labor that Heracles faced was kidnapping Cerberus, a three-headed hound that guarded the entrance to the underworld. In most stories, this gigantic beast had a dragon's tail and its back was lined with snake heads.

Before he ventured to the underworld, Heracles made sure that he took extra precautions. He knew that this will be the toughest labor that he will face, considering that it was a journey from which no mortal had ever returned. Heracles had a feeling that he cannot escape Hades' wrath once he ventured into the underworld, so he first visited Eumolpus, a priest who lived in Eleusis. This priest was known for the Eleusinian mysteries. It was believed that people who discovered these mysteries would find happiness and good luck when they entered the Underworld.

After uncovering these mysteries, Heracles travelled to Taenarum. He entered a rocky cave and descended into the underworld.

During his visit to the land of the dead, the hero faced a lot of monsters, dead heroes, and ghosts. He even had another wrestling match with one of the souls. Afterwards, he went to Hades and requested for Cerberus. The god of the dead allowed Heracles to take the dog—that is, if he could defeat the beast using his own brute strength.

Heracles found the three-headed dog at the gates of Acheron. Without fear, the hero attacked the beast and wrestled him using his muscular arms. The dog bit Heracles, but he didn't flinch. He was so strong that Cerberus admitted defeat.

Heracles brought the beast to Eurystheus. But similar to the apples of Hesperides, Cerberus was returned back to Hades.

After finishing the 12 labors, Heracles didn't retire from adventuring. One of his most popular quests was rescuing the princess of Troy from the clutches of a sea monster. His strength was also used to help Zeus defeat a giant that wanted to take control over Olympus.

In addition, Heracles also married for the second time. His new wife was Deianira, a beautiful damsel. She was quite skilled with weaving, so she gave him a magical cloak as a welcome present after coming home from his quest.

Deianira imbued this cloak with a special balm. According to the centaur who gave her this item, Heracles would love her forever once he applied this balm on his skin. Deianira was afraid that her husband was having an affair with other women during his journey, so she lathered a large amount of this balm on the cloak to make sure that he remained loyal to her forever.

What she didn't know was that the balm actually contained a potent, caustic poison. So when Heracles wore the cloak, an unbearable, burning pain spread all over his body. He removed the cloak, but the fast-acting poison was already buried deep within his skin. Since he was immortal, he must endure this poison forever. He decided that dying would be better than experiencing eternal agony.

Heracles asked his friends to create a large pyre on top of Mount Oeta. The Greek hero laid himself on top of the funeral pyre and instructed his friends to ignite it.

The gods were looking down on top of Mount Olympus as the funeral was starting. Then, Zeus ordered Athena to bring his son to Olympus using her chariot. Heracles was healed from his injuries and he was allowed to stay there for the rest of his days.

Atlanta

The Greek Mythology is not just filled with tales of strong and powerful men. Women also had their moment of glory in the world of mythology. One of the most renowned female heroines of all time was Atlanta.

Little is known about her parentage. It was said that her father was King Iasus and her mother was Clymene. During her time, being a woman was difficult because they were not deemed to be as strong as men.

When she was still a baby, her father left her in the middle of the woods and left her there to die. Thankfully, a bear found little Atlanta and took her as her own. As she grew up, she interacted with a lot of hunters and she learned a lot from them. Just like Artemis, she enjoyed hunting and going outdoors.

Atlanta was a free-spirited woman who believed that she does not need a man in his life. An oracle even told her that her marriage would only end in tragedy.

This heroine was very fierce when it comes to protecting her virginity. Two centaurs once attempted to rape her, but she just killed them both using her arrows.

She wanted to join the Argonauts before. However, Jason believed that bringing a woman with them on this journey would only bring a terrible fate to the whole crew.

Atlanta was very skilled when it comes to using her bow and arrow. In fact, she was the one who drew first blood during the Calydonian Boar Hunt.

After some time, her father sought forgiveness from his daughter and asked her to come back to his kingdom. When Atlanta arrived, the king performed his fatherly duties of finding her a husband. Fearing any dangerous resentment, Atlanta did not blatantly refuse her father's help. Instead, she proposed a challenge to her suitors. In order to win her hand, a suitor must be able to beat her in a foot race. In addition, the losing suitors will be beheaded by Atlanta herself. She was one of the fastest mortals around, so it was deemed impossible for any man to beat her.

Her plan worked for several years. In some cases, she would even wear heavy armor just to give a handicap advantage to her suitors. In some stories, she was even generous enough to give them a head start. However, Atlanta always won the race.

There was, however, one suitor who managed to beat her. Melanion wanted to win Atlanta's love, but he was afraid that he would lose the race. So what he did was he prayed to Aphrodite. The goddess of love had a weakness for such tragedies, and she was greatly concerned that the heroine was rejecting and killing so many of her suitors.

Aphrodite helped Melanion by giving him three golden apples. He carried these fruits during the race, and every time Atlanta caught up to him, he would just throw an apple on the ground. In the eyes of Atlanta, this magic fruit was totally irresistible. She would spend some time in picking up the apple and looking at its shiny surface.

Melanion kept throwing the golden apples every time Atlanta would catch up to him. In the end, he managed to win the race.

Even though Atlanta detested marriage in the past, it worked out just fine for her. Her husband was so overjoyed with his victory that he forgot his promise to sacrifice to Aphrodite. And just like in any other story, people who forgot to thank the gods ended up getting severely punished.

While the couple was passing by the shrine of a god, Aphrodite struck them with intense passion, and both mortals decided to make love inside the shrine. The god was offended with this act and turned them both into lions.

Perseus

According to Greek legends, there was a king called Acrisius and he had a daughter named Danae. An oracle once told the king that her daughter's son would kill him. Fearing for his own life, he locked up Danae in a bronze tower so no mortal man could come near her.

The bronze tower does not have any door, save for a small window. Being in isolation for such a long time made her feel sad. One day, a ray of golden light entered through the window. Then, a handsome man who was holding a thunderbolt appeared right in front of her.

Danae knew that her visitor was no ordinary mortal, but she doesn't know his real identity. The god offered to become her husband and turn her dark prison into a beautiful field.

Just like what the deity said, her prison became as wonderful as the Elsysian Fields. One day, Acrisius saw light coming out from the tower's window, so he asked his guards to investigate. When the guards tore down one side of the wall, they saw Danae holding a baby in her hands. The king was furious with this discovery. He placed Danae and her baby inside a huge chest and threw them out to the sea.

By some miracle, they survived the horrible ordeal and drifted towards the isle of Seriphos. The ruler of the land was Polydectes. Dictys, a fisherman and brother of the king, caught the huge chest where the mother and son were locked up.

Over the years, Perseus grew up to become strong and healthy. Polydectes wanted to marry Danae, but she rejected his advances. The king feared that Perseus will kill him if he took her mother by force, so he created a plan to get rid of him.

The king pretended to marry his friend's daughter, and everyone in the city needed to bring a gift. Perseus was a poor man, so he wasn't able to give anything to the king. Polydectes pretended to be angry with the young man. To avoid the wrath of the king, Perseus told Polydectes that he will give him anything he wants. Afterwards, the king asked Perseus to bring him the head of Gorgon Medusa.

The young hero embarked on his quest. He wandered several lands for days, searching in vain for the Gorgon's hidden lair. Perseus searched for Medusa in an unknown city. There, he discovered how horrible that monster was. Medusa was known for her hair made of snakes and her horrible gaze that could turn anyone who looked back at her into stone.

Suddenly, two divine beings appeared right before him. One was a tall woman while the other one was a young man wearing winged sandals. The deities introduced themselves as Athena and Hermes. The messenger god informed Perseus that the three of them were brothers, considering that their father was Zeus. Hermes gave the mortal hero his flying sandals and sickle, while Athena gave him her shield so he could look at Medusa without gazing directly into her eyes. They also told him where to find the Gorgon.

Afterwards, Perseus travelled to the cave of the Graeae. These were three old women who shared a single eyeball. The young hero stole their eye, and coerced them to help him with his quest. The Graeae told him to search for the Northern nymphs and grab the Cap of Darkness, a magical item that can render anyone invisible.

Once Perseus got the items he needed, it was time to hunt Medusa. With the Cap of Darkness, he turned himself invisible and killed Medusa. Even when the Gorgon was dead, her eyes could still petrify anyone. Perseus used the shield to pick up the head from the ground and placed it in a magical bag.

Medusa's sisters suddenly woke up and attempted to attack Perseus. However, the young hero escaped using Hermes' flying sandals.

While he was travelling back to Seriphus, he met Atlas. In order to free him from the burden of lifting the sky, he turned the Titan to stone. That way, he won't feel any pain while lifting the sky on his shoulders.

Perseus also married Andromeda and saved her from her punishment. He first saw the lady chained to a rock. Andromeda told Perseus her name and the reason why she was chained up. The young hero discovered she was punished for her mother's crime. Andromeda's mother boasted that she was more beautiful compared to the Nereids or sea nymphs. This brash statement greatly angered Poseidon, the god of the sea. Afterwards, the god took Andromeda and sacrificed her to a sea monster.

The monster rose from the depths of the sea while they were talking. Perseus pulled out the Gorgon's head from his bag and then showed it to the monster. The savage creature immediately turned to stone and then crumbled away. Then, Perseus freed Andromeda from her bonds and returned her to Phoenicia, where King Cepheus, her father, was waiting. The young hero asked for his daughter's hand, and the king happily allowed them to get married. Afterwards, the new couple headed off to Seriphus to bring the Gorgon's head to King Polydectes.

He also visited Larisa wherein he competed in several games. In the discus competition, he threw a flying disc and accidentally hit an old man, who died instantly after getting hit with the disc. Little did Perseus know that he had just killed his grandfather Acrisisus. Therefore, the prophecy of the oracle came true.

When they reached the island of Seriphus, they were greeted by Dictys. The old man told Perseus and Andromeda that Polydectes had forced Danae to marry him. His mother greatly rejected the offer, so she was turned into the king's handmaiden instead. The young hero was angry with what Polydectes had done to his mother. Then, he ordered Dictys to take him to the palace.

When Perseus saw the king, he immediately raised the Gorgon's head. Everyone inside the court instantly turned into stone. Perseus,

Andromeda, and Danae lived happily after that. In addition, the couple gave birth to powerful kings.

Perseus died in the hands of Dionysus. The gods immortalized the fallen hero and his wife by turning them into bright stars.

Bellerophon

If there's one thing that you can learn from the life of Bellerophon, it's that one should establish good relationships with the gods to assure a safe journey. He was a model hero because at a young age, he already knew how to honor the gods. Sadly, his pride led him to his own demise.

The parents of Bellerophon were Poseidon and Eurynome. However, the one who raised him up was Glaucus, Eurynome's other mortal husband. Glaucus did not know that Bellerophon was the son of Poseidon, so he accepted him with open arms. Both of the hero's fathers were very interested in horses (It was said that Poseidon was the one who created the horses, along with its other brethren such as the zebra, giraffe, etc.). This meant that Bellorophon must also have the same interest as them.

Sadly, he did not inherit the skill to ride a horse. So in order to overcome this hurdle, he sought help from Polyeidus. The man told him that he should spend one night inside Athena's sacred temple. While he was sleeping, he had a strange dream wherein the goddess of wisdom gave him a golden bridle that was brimming with magic. When he woke up, he was surprised that the bridle was in his hands.

When morning came, Bellerophon instinctively offered a sacrifice to Athena and Poseidon. This was one of the traits that made him a favorite amongst the gods and goddesses. Then, he travelled to the meadow where the flying horse, Pegasus, was frequently grazing.

After placing the bridle on the magical horse, he managed to tame it effortlessly. He was happy with what he had accomplished, so he visited King Pittheus and asked if he can marry one of his daughters, Aethra. But in a cruel twist of fate, he killed a man right before they got married. This caused him to be banished from the kingdom forever.

Next, Bellerophon visited the nearby kingdom that was ruled by King Proetus. He asked to be pardoned for his crimes, and the king obliged. The king also allowed the hero to stay in his house. While Bellorophon was still living under King Proteus' care, the Queen Stheneboea tried to seduce him. Since the Greek hero was noble and righteous, he did not give in to temptation and blocked off her advances. This made the queen furious and she told her husband that Bellorophon was the one who was seducing her.

Since the hero committed a crime before, King Proteus was greatly upset by this news and he wanted the hero to be banished from his castle. However, he also does not want to create a huge public scandal. In addition, harming a guest in your very own home was considered a grave offense to the gods and goddesses, especially Hera. So what King Proteus did was he gave the hero a sealed letter and asked him to deliver it to King Iobates, the father of Queen Stheneboea.

Bellerophon arrived at King Iobates' doorstep. Just like in the previous castle, he was greeted warmly and was considered as an honorable guest. The hero gave King Iobates the sealed letter from King Proteus. When he opened it, he discovered his daughter's accusations against Bellerophon.

In order to get rid of the hero without offending the gods, he made Bellerophon embark on a series of dangerous heroic quests.

Bellorophon was a skilled archer and he was also very brave. In addition, his flying horse Pegasus gave him a superb advantage over his enemies because he could snipe them from the skies. There were also a lot of other factors why he could overcome such dangerous tasks. This included his parentage and his unique relationship with the deities.

In his adventures, he managed to kill a Chimaera, defeat the Solymi tribe, and fight the Amazons.

King Iobates was so desperate in getting rid of Bellerophon that he planned to ambush him using his entire army. Unluckily, all of his men were killed by the hero.

This made the king realize that something is definitely not right with the hero's situation. Iobates learned that the gods favor Bellerophon more because he honored them properly.

The king made amends to the young hero by giving him half of his kingdom, some his best farmlands, and even his daughter, Philonoe.

There were several stories regarding the fate of Stheneboea, the queen who falsely accused Bellerophon of sexual harassment. Some stories said that the hero made her ride Pegasus and the horse shove her to her death. Others said that the queen committed suicide.

For many years, the hero and his wife lived happily. His amazing adventures were sung throughout the land, and he was blessed with two daughters and two sons. He was a righteous king, so his people loved him greatly.

Sadly, Bellerophon became greedy over time. He became arrogant enough to believe that he could actually fly Pegasus to Mount Olympus and pay a visit to the gods. Zeus was not willing to let boastful demigods enter his home, so he sent a gadfly to sting Pegasus. The horse panicked in the air and he accidentally threw Bellerophon off his seat. Although the hero survived the fall, he remained crippled for the rest of his life. He also lost his kingdom and was forced to roam the earth on his own. No one was willing to help him because he greatly offended the gods.

Monsters and Fantastic Mythological Creatures

Monsters are essential in the lives of many a Greek hero. Facing these enemies made them strong and it also helped them become more famous.

However, one should remember that not all creatures in Greek Mythology are fierce and savage. Some are also compassionate, and they've even helped other heroes on their quests. Here are the some of the most prominent monsters and creatures in the realm of Greek myth.

Argus Panoptes

More popularly called as Argos, this giant was known for its one hundred eyes scattered around its body. His second name, Panoptes, is the Greek term for "all-seeing one." He served Hera in the past, and one of his tasks was to kill the creature Echidna – the wife of the Titan Typhon. He was also asked by Hera to watch over Io, one of the nymphs who had an affair with Zeus.

It's very difficult to escape when Argos is watching you, considering that his body is covered with a hundred eyes. So what Zeus did was that he asked Hermes to disguise himself as a shepherd. Using his skills in music, Hermes made Argos go to sleep. When all of the giant's eyes were closed, the messenger god bashed his head with a stone.

Centaur

A centaur is a creature with both human and horse-like features. They have the limbs and body of a horse, while their arms, chest, head, and torso are those of a human's. According to legend, these creatures populated the earth thanks to the union of a single Centaurus and the Magnesian mares.

The most popular centaur in Greek mythology was Chiron. While most of his kind was depicted as lustful and unruly, Chiron was portrayed as the wisest and kindest of them all. Out of all the other centaurs, he was the most civilized and well-read. In fact, Chiron has impressive skills in medicine and teaching.

During his time, a lot of Greek mythological characters went under his tutelage, including Achilles and Aesculapius.

Chiron was an immortal creature. However, that did not prevent him from experiencing great pain. Heracles once shot him with an arrow dipped in the Hydra's poison. To free himself from this excruciating pain, he offered to sacrifice his life to the gods.

Chimera

Similar to Centaurs, the Chimera is also a hybrid creature. However, the difference is that the Chimera is a combination of more than just two beasts. As the cousin of Cerberus and Hydra, this creature has the head and the body of a lion. In addition, it also has a goat's head placed on its back. The end of its tail, meanwhile, is a snake. The Chimaera also has wings, allowing it to grab its enemies and then drop them off at a considerable height.

The Chimera lived most of its life in Lycia. Using its fiery breath, the beast ravaged the people's homes and killed everyone who crossed its path. Its reign of terror was ended by Bellerophon and the winged horse, Pegasus.

Cyclops

These creatures are known as one-eyed giants. One of the most popular Cyclops in Greek mythology was Polyphemus, the monster that captured Odysseus and ate his crew. Most of these creatures were the sons of Uranus and Gaea, two of the most powerful Titans. However, the father of Polyphemus was Poseidon, god of the sea.

Similar to the earth giants, Cyclops are also wild creatures with massive strength. They don't follow any laws or social manners. In addition, they do not fear the gods and goddesses. They are highly resistant to heat, making them the perfect workers for Hephaestus. The smith god crafts his magical weapons in the heart of Etna, an active volcano. In addition, these Cyclops have also helped in crafting Zeus' thunderbolt.

Giants

Giants are a separate race from the Cyclopes. According to legends, giants were formed after the blood of the Titan Uranus fell on the earth and hit the Titan goddess, Gaea. These massive and strong monsters fought alongside the Titans during the great Titanomachy, which is probably one of the most important battles between the gods.

Some of the most well-known giants in the Greek mythology are:

- **Enceladus** – He was crushed under the island of Sicily during the Great War.
- **Eurymedon** – He was known as the king of the Giants. It was said that he raped Hera and his son was Prometheus, the Titan who gave fire to the humans.
- **Porphyrin** – He was one of the most powerful giant in the land. He was only killed when Zeus struck him a thunderbolt.

Hecatoncheires

In Greece, the name Hecatoncheires means "hundred-handed ones." In addition to their one hundred hands, these giant-like creatures also have fifty heads. Their parents were Uranus and Gaea. There were only three known Hecatoncheires: Briareus, the vigorous sea goat, Cottus, the furious one, and Gyges, the huge-limbed.

These three hundred-handed monsters represent the destructive power of earthquakes and tidal waves.

During the Titanomachy, these giants proved to be great allies to the gods. Using their hands, they threw huge boulders at their enemies and defended Mount Olympus.

Silenus

This creature was the most favorite companion of Dionysus, the god of wine and merriment. He was considered as the oldest satyr in the land. However, his physical features made him look more like a horse rather than a goat.

Aside from Silenus, Dionysus also had other followers, and they were known as Sileni. Their most common characteristic is that they were always drunk. The satyr Silenus gained immense arcane knowledge whenever he was under the influence of wine. There were also instances wherein he was able to predict the future.

Minotaur

As mentioned in the previous chapter, a Minotaur is a grotesque monster that has the head of a bull and a body of a human. The monster was trapped inside a labyrinth which was under King Minos' palace in Crete.

Every year, the king would sacrifice seven maidens and seven boys to the Minotaur to prevent the beast from waging war against the Athenians. The Minotaur was killed by the Greek hero, Theseus.

The Titanomachy

In Greek Mythology, the Titanomachy refers to the ten year battle between the Titans (the older pantheon of gods residing in Mount Othyrs), and the Greek gods (the newer generation that reigned on Mount Olympus). The series of battles were all fought in Thessaly. There were a lot of names for this great event. It was also called as The Titan War, Battle of the Gods, or the War of the Titans.

The battle was fought in order to decide which pantheon would reign over the entire universe. In the end, the victory went to the Olympian gods.

In the beginning

Before the Greek Olympian gods sprang into existence, the universe was ruled by Uranus, the supreme Titan lord. His wife was Gaea, and their children were the Cyclopes, other Titans, and the hundred-handed giants. Gaea became furious over Uranus because he incarcerated his children and sent them to Tartarus, the lowest depths of the earth.

One day, Gaea conspired with her youngest son, Cronos, to thwart Uranus. Gaea formed a powerful sickle that could kill her husband, and she also called Cronos' other siblings so they can castrate their father. Since Cronos was the only one brave enough to do this task, her mother gave him the sickle.

The younger Titan ambushed his father while he was talking to Gaea. Using the sickle, he cut off Uranus' genitals and threw them in the sea. The blood from his genitals mixed with the salt water, creating the thick foam that formed into a beautiful maiden. This was how Aphrodite was born.

Castrating his father made Cronos the new king of the Titans. But upon Uranus' defeat, he made a prophecy that one day, the children of Cronos will gather together and thwart him. The younger Titan paid no heed to his father's prophecy. He dispatched Uranus and locked away his other siblings so that they won't have the chance to remove him from his throne.

To make sure that his father's prophecy won't come true, Cronos swallowed his sons and daughters every time his wife, Rhea, would give birth. Since his children were also immortals, they did not die when Cronos ate them. Instead, they grew inside his belly.

When Cronos was about to eat Zeus, the youngest child, Rhea tricked her husband by giving him a rock swaddled in a blanket. She also sought help from her parents, Gaea and Uranus. The older Titans showed her the future and helped them create a plan to beat Cronos.

Afterwards, Rhea hid Zeus in one of the caves in Crete. The young god was raised by Amalthea, a goat. According to legends, Amalthea's horn may have been the cornucopia, or the horn of plenty. When Zeus grew into an adult, he pretended to be Cronos' cup bearer. He gained the Titan's trust, and he became his father's personal servant.

With the help of Metis, Zeus managed to give his father a concoction that will make him vomit his own children. This special drink was made from wine mixed with mustard. When his brothers and sisters were freed, Zeus started his plan to take the throne of his father.

The Great Titan War

There were no historical records that told what immediately happened after Cronos vomited his children. The stories skipped when the Titanomachy began.

For ten years, the Titans and Olympians clashed fiercely with no clear victories on both sides. In Greek mythology, a decade was the traditional period for an extremely long war. The younger gods were in Mount Olympus, while the Titans were in Mount Othyrs. In the middle of the two mountains was Thessaly, the northern part of Greece.

The gods and Titans were both immortal, so they cannot really harm themselves. However, the younger pantheon gained the upper hand by seeking aid from ancient creatures that were locked up in Tartarus.

Upon Gaea's advice, Zeus freed the hundred-handed ones and the Cyclopes that were imprisoned in Tartarus. The sky god promised them a reward if they helped him defeat his father. The Cyclopes forged Zeus' thunderbolt, giving him a powerful weapon that can incinerate his foes. Afterwards, they also built Poseidon's magical trident and Hades' sacred helmet.

The hundred-handed ones, meanwhile, provided both offense and defense during the battle. They sent a barrage of huge boulders at the Titans' path, making it difficult for them to reach Mount Olympus.

With the immense power of the ancient creatures, other gods, and Zeus' thunderbolt, the Titans were finally defeated after ten years. Afterwards, they were sent to Tartarus, and the hundred-handed ones became their jail wardens.

Aftermath of the Titan War

While most of the Titans were imprisoned in Tartarus, some of them were given unique punishments. An example of this one was Atlas. As one of the leaders during the Titanomachy, he was ordered by the Olympians to carry the weight of the sky on his shoulders for the rest of his life.

Prometheus, meanwhile, was pardoned because of his intelligence and kind nature. However, he was also punished by the gods when he gave the gift of fire to mortals. He was chained up on a mountain and every day, an eagle would swoop down and eat his liver. Since he was immortal, the liver would grow back, and the eagle would swoop down again. This agonizing torture continued until Heracles removed him from his bonds.

The female Titans, meanwhile, were not imprisoned because they did not directly participate in the fighting. Instead, Themis, Mnemosyne, and Metis became the mothers of the Muses and the Horai.

After their overwhelming victory against the Titans, the brothers Poseidon, Zeus, and Hades divided the world amongst themselves. Zeus, the youngest of the three, became the lord of the sky and air.

Poseidon became the lord of the seas. Hades, on the other hand, handled the Underworld. They were also given special powers so they could rule each of their domains more effectively. The earth, meanwhile, became a common ground for all the gods and they were allowed to do anything with it.

The Trojan War

Have you ever heard of the term *"a face that launched a thousand ships?"* No? Well, this particular quote was dedicated to Helen of Troy, one of the most beautiful women who ever walked the earth—at least according to Greek legend. In fact, she was so beautiful that a war was waged between two powerful countries when she got kidnapped.

The Trojan War was a conflict between the Greeks and the Trojans in western Anatolia. According to scholars, this event happened way back during the 13th century BC. The Greeks were utterly fascinated by the Trojan War, and it was even celebrated in various other stories such as the Iliad and Homer's Odyssey. There were a lot of other earlier written works pertaining to this battle, but many of them were lost.

The Beginning of the War

In the past, the kingdom of Troy was ruled by King Priam. Aside from being financially prosperous, this ruler was also blessed to have more than fifty children. Each of his sons and daughters also inherited his good fortune.

But one night, his wife Hecuba dreamed that she gave birth to a firebrand. Her prophets interpreted this nightmare and told her that her unborn son will cause the downfall of Troy. When the baby was born, his parents left him on top of Mount Ida. A she-bear found the infant and raised him as her own. He grew up to be a shepherd and called himself Paris.

Somewhere in Greece, Peleus and his new wife Thetis were enjoying their wedding anniversary. Eris wanted to cause mischief during the event, so she threw a golden apple in the air and said, "To the fairest."

Three goddesses claimed that the apple was hers: Hera, Athena, and Aphrodite. Zeus did not want to incur the wrath of these deities, so he instructed them to visit Paris and ask who's the fairest of them all.

The goddesses offered the shepherd several gifts to win his favor. Hera offered to turn him into a noble king who would rule over Asia. Athena, meanwhile, promised him superb intelligence and invincibility in warfare.

However, Aphrodite won Paris' favor when she offered Helen, the most beautiful woman on Earth. Although he made a good choice, little did Paris know that he had just incurred the wrath of two powerful goddesses. Athena and Hera both promised that they would destroy Troy when they had the chance. Another problem that Paris encountered was that Helen was already married to the Spartan King Menelaus.

So in order to gain reinforcements, Paris first visited Troy and declared that he was also King Priam's son. Afterwards, he went to Sparta and seduced Helen. While her husband was away, the couple snuck off and went back to Troy.

In Paris' hometown, his sister Cassandra was in a big dilemma. Apollo got angry at her for not submitting to his advances. As punishment, the god gave her a curse. She would be able to see the future, but no one would believe her. She was the one who saw through Paris' lust, as well as the impending doom that he would bring upon the land.

King Priam disregarded his daughter's warnings and locked Cassandra up in a cell.

The return of Menelaus

When Menelaus returned to his kingdom, he was furious that his wife was nowhere to be seen. He knew that Paris was the one who took his wife, so he summoned all the Spartan chieftains and drafted a war plan against Troy. These chieftains rallied under Agamemnon, Menelaus' brother.

While most of the Greek heroes were excited to conquer Troy, there were two warriors who were not enthusiastic with the task: Odysseus and Achilles. An oracle once told Odysseus that when he joins the war, it will take him two decades before he can return home. He tried to fake his madness just to escape his fate, but it didn't work.

Achilles, meanwhile, didn't want to join the war because he was afraid that he would live a short life. However, the Greeks did not accept this reason, considering that he was a skilled fighter. In addition, his nymph mother Thetis made him bathe in the River Styx, making him invulnerable during a fight.

After a long journey, the Greeks finally arrived in Trojan territory. The first Greek soldier who stepped on the land of Troy was immediately killed by Hector, one of Paris' older brothers and the mightiest hero in the land.

The Battle

The gods also participated in this event. Mount Olympus became divided into two factions. Apollo, Artemis, Ares, and Aphrodite allied with the Trojans, while the remaining deities, Hera, Athena, Poseidon, Hephaestus, and Hermes, sided with the Greeks. The god of thunder also wanted to participate, but he decided to remain neutral to ensure balance.

The Trojan War dragged on for nine years. Even though the Greeks destroyed some of the enemy forces in Asia Minor, they did not make a lot of headway. The kingdom of Troy was powerful, but the internal strife among the Greeks was also the cause of their defeat.

First, Odysseus framed Palamedes, another warrior, and blamed him for the recent failure of the foraging expedition. As a result, the warrior was stoned to death.

Next, Achilles fought Agamemnon because the leader of the chieftains took his concubine. Afterwards, Achilles refused to help out in the war. The Myrmidons, his followers, also quit fighting. With such a powerful force gone from the battlefield, it became easier for Troy to destroy the Greek army.

It also did not help that Zeus ordered the other gods to return to Mount Olympus. With the deities gone, Hector led the Trojans in several victorious assaults.

Patroclus, one of Achilles' men, became alarmed by what was happening to the Greek army. Wishing to raise his comrades' crushed spirits, he disguised himself, pretending to be Achilles, and led the Greeks into battle. This gave the army a sense of hope and strength. They fought bravely until Patroclus was killed by Hector and the whole Greek army discovered that it was not Achilles who led them. With their leader gone, it was difficult for the army to maintain their composure.

Achilles heard the news, and he was overcome by grief at the loss of his great warrior and friend. In his fury, he took his armor and sword and then joined the battle.

When Achilles returned to the battlefield, the war became more favorable to the Greeks in no time at all. The hero was powerful and unbeatable. Hector and Aeneas slew a lot of enemies, but Achilles killed more.

Hector fought Achilles outside the walls of Troy. At first, it seemed that Hector was gaining the upper hand. But then, Achilles saw an opening and rammed a lance in his opponent's throat, killing him. In his anger, he tied Hector's corpse to a chariot and dragged him around the city.

The death of Hector filled the Trojans' hearts with fear and sadness. Priam saw how his son's body was dragged around the kingdom, and he almost died of grief. So in order to retrieve his son's body, he lowered his pride and infiltrated the enemy camp where Achilles was staying. He begged the Greek hero to give Hector's body back. Achilles felt pity upon the old man, so he gave in to the king's pleas. In addition, Achilles also announced a temporary truce so the Trojans can mourn for their fallen hero.

When the truce was over, the hostilities resumed. During one of the battles, Paris managed to kill Achilles. He shot an arrow in the air, and Apollo guided it so it can land onto the hero's only vulnerable spot – his heel.

The Greeks felt hopeless after losing two of their heroes. However, Odysseus had a plan. The army created a large, wooden horse and offered it as a sacrifice to the Trojans. The king accepted the gift and everyone celebrated their victory. When night came, the Greek warriors hiding inside the wooden horse came out and ravaged the city. No one in Troy saw that coming, so they were defeated easily.

Creation Myths

When the universe was still young, there was nothing but Chaos. And after many years, the void was shattered and Erebus was created. This was a place where death and Night can be found. As such, the land of Erebus was lonely, dark, and silent.

By some miracle, Love and Order were born from this endlessly dark place. Love gave birth to Light, Gaea, and finally, the earth.

Erebus and Night also gave birth to Ether, a heavenly form of light. Afterwards, Night gave birth to Doom, Nemesis, Fate, Sleep, Dream, and other entities that lurk in the darkness.

Gaea, on the other hand, created Uranus. Both beings created a relationship and gave birth to three powerful Cyclopes, three Hundred-handed giants, and twelve Titans.

Uranus was a very terrifying father to his children. He despised the hundred-handed giants, so he locked them away in the deepest parts of the Earth. This made Gaea furious, and she swore that she would avenge her children.

Gaea created a sickle and asked for her sons to kill Uranus. None of them were willing to try, save for Cronos, the youngest Titan. Gaea and her son ambushed Uranus. After capturing him, Cronos castrated his father and threw his genitals into the ocean.

When Uranus was castrated, his blood soaked the earth, creating other creatures such as the Ash Tree Nymphs, the Furies, and the race of giants.

Cronos became the next ruler, and he became as bad as his father. He sent his other brother in Tartaros and married Rhea, his sister. The couple gave birth to the gods and goddesses, who, in turn, overthrew him during the great Titan War.

Gaea became furious with Zeus and the other gods because they imprisoned her beloved Titans. So what she did was she gave birth to Typhon, the very last Titan to ravage the earth. He may be the youngest in the Titan race, but he was the most powerful being that the Gods ever faced. Typhon was known as the Father of Monsters for he created several terrifying creatures such as the Sphinx, the Nemean Lion, and Cerberus to name a few.

The Creation of the Human Race

The gods thought that it's interesting to create beings that are shaped in their own image and likeness. Zeus created the human beings from gold, bronze, and even soil. This gave the mortals varying appearances.

Afterwards, the god of lightning asked the Titans Prometheus, Iapetus, and Epimetheus to provide their gifts to the human race. This was to make sure that the mortals became more interesting.

Epimetheus gave beauty, agility, strength, and speed to various creatures. However, he made sure that the mortals were defenseless. Prometheus, meanwhile, gave man reasoning and fire. He also taught the humans everything that he knew. This angered the gods, so they punished him greatly.

Archeological Sources

The modern world was able to enjoy the epic stories of gods and heroes because the Greek myths were recorded in various artifacts.

Usually, these myths were found in ancient poems. Two of the oldest poems known to mankind were the Iliad and the Odyssey. They were both created by Homer during the 8th century BC. However, scholars believed that these masterpieces were already recorded as oral history, even before Homer wrote them on paper.

Aside from the poems, researchers also found epics such as Apollonius Rhodius' Argonautica that tells the adventures of Jason and his Argonauts. These were created during the third century BC. Pindar, a Greek poet, also composed odes that refer to ancient myths. He commemorated most of his work to the Olympic champions of his time.

The dramatists Aeschylus, Sophocles, and Euripedes used these myths to create their plays.

These myths are very adaptable, which means that they do not really have a definite form. Each poet, singer, or playwright is free to use these tales and mold their shape depending on their needs. Some changes can be minor, while other ones can be extensive. An example of this one was Euripedes' version of Helen of Troy. The writer wanted Helen to become a character with which everyone can sympathize. So what he did was he placed Helen in Egypt and made it look like she had nothing to do with the Trojan War.

The beauty about tweaking myths is that it invokes a new idea to the audience. However, the challenge here is that the writers need to make it culturally relevant so that it will not be meaningless.

Hesiod's Theogony and Works and Days

Perhaps one of the biggest contributors of immortalizing the Greek myth was Hesiod's two works—Theogony and the Works and Days. These were different sets of genealogies that were filled with etiological legends and folktales.

Both masterpieces are like diptychs, meaning that they are dependent on each other. The poem Theogony tells the identities of the gods. The other one, meanwhile, provides some useful pieces of advice on how to survive in a world filled with horrible creatures.

Other Literary Sources of Greek Mythology

Callimachus, a poet and scholar from Alexandria, developed some of the most obscure myths. His main mythographer was Euhemerus. According to him, the gods were really human. This school of thought was known as Euhemerism.

Even the Romans also played a great role in preserving the Greek myths. Examples of their literary contributions were the Geography of Strabo and the Library of the pseudo Apollodrous. Plutarch and Hygnius also transferred the Greek mythology in Latin.

Archaeological Sources of the Greek Myth

Some of the most vital sources of Greek mythology came from German archaeologist Heinrich Schliemann. He was the one who discovered the hidden civilization of Mycenae and the Minoan culture in Crete. Because of his work, scholars learned more about the Greek rituals. This discovery also helped the modern scholars to better understand the Minoan and Mycenaean cultures.

Some of the Greek potteries were also designed with scenes from the Trojan War, as well as the exciting adventures of Heracles. However, the style of storytelling was too formal, making it difficult to identify the characters.

The country of Greece was also replete with shrines and other religious places of worship. This includes the Temple of Zeus—a set of monolithic ruins found in Athens. Even though the columns were the only parts of this temple that remain standing to this day, one can easily determine that the original structure was huge. The temple was built during the 2nd century AD.

Poseidon, god of the sea, also has his own temple at Sounion. It was created around 440 BC, and the columns of the structure were dated from the Archaic Era. Similar to the Temple of Zeus, only the columns remained of this massive structure. However, the temple is still teeming with an air of mystery and beauty. The temple of Poseidon is located near the sea, so the breeze is fresh and very relaxing. This place of worship looks very similar to the Hephaestus temple which is located in the Acropolis.

The Influence of Greek Mythology on the Modern World

Even though the Greek myths are centuries old, it does not mean that they cannot contribute in today's society. In fact, these stories and poems have an impact in our present culture; it's just that this impact is not widely known to us.

Thanks to the Greek culture, people are now enjoying the benefits of democracy, mathematics, architecture, and even the alphabet. Even without using any modern tools, they managed to build monoliths and structures that can withstand the test of time.

The Greek myths have affected the modern society in a manner that's a little bit different from what Greece did for the world as a whole.

A great example of this one was the Olympic Games. In the past, these sporting events were not just about winning the gold medal. The Olympics were actually an event dedicated to Zeus, the sky father. Other sporting events dedicated to different gods included the Pythian Games for Apollo and the Isthmian games for Poseidon. The old and modern Olympics both held the tradition of giving a crown made of olive leaves during the opening and closing ceremonies.

The stories about gods, heroes, and monsters also have an impact on architecture. In the past, Greece was filled with various temples and shrines for worshipping the gods and goddesses. Since they were made for the divine beings, the Greeks made sure that they were built beautifully. The Romans even adapted Greek architecture, even after invading the country.

Even if you have not read the original Greek versions of the myths, you will still fall in love with the amazing stories of valor and adventure. Because these tales are timeless classics, they were adapted into several movies, books, and television shows. What's more, artists also used these old stories as inspiration for their new tales, poems, or other works of art. A great example of this one was Rick Riordan's *Percy Jackson* novels. This series of books tells the story of demigods who are living in the modern world. It's a little bit different from the original Greek myths, but people still became interested in these works of art.

The Greek myths even found a way to influence the field of psychology. Examples of these are the Oedipal complex and the Elektra complex. The former concept refers to children who love their mother, but extremely hate their father. The latter concept, meanwhile, is the opposite. The Oedipal complex came from the story of Oedipus. In this tale, he killed his father and had an affair with his mother. The Elektra complex came from the myth of Elektra. This lady was a princess and daughter of King Agamemnon. She swore revenge against her mother, Queen Clytemnestra, for leaving her family.

Language was another area that was also influenced by the Greek myths. The word arachnid, for example, became the medical term for spider. Arachnid came from the story of Arachne, the woman who turned into a spider because of her pride.

The 12 Gods of Olympus

Believed to have been benevolent beings that presided over humanity, Greek gods were portrayed to have very human flaws and characteristics. This, in turn, gave rise to many conflicts and stories that consequently gave birth to many legends and epics that comprised the whole of Greek mythology.

Atop the high mountains of Olympus, the gods dwelled and enjoyed their reign over mankind. 12 children of the Titans who conquered their own predecessors sat comfortably within the confines of their palace. Each god held dominion over a certain aspect of Greek life, giving each deity a certain responsibility and personality.

Interestingly, different stories from Greek papers depict different sets of gods that resided on mount Olympus. To bring about a general total, 14 gods have been known to have resided in the palace of the gods.

Aphrodite

Known as the goddess of love and sex, Aphrodite was indeed very much involved in multiple affairs of romance. Patronage to her was symbolized by a dove, scallop and an apple.

Interestingly, she wasn't born from the union of any two titans. In fact, she came from the murderous affair Cronus committed against Uranus. In an attempt to dethrone his father, Cronus castrated Uranus and threw his testicles into the sea. There, it combined with the salt and foam. From there, Aphrodite came to be. Such was her birth that grass grew from her feet as she stepped on land.

Being the goddess of love, it comes as no surprise that she was found to love, and have been loved by many beings. Most scandalous of her affairs was her liaison with Ares, the god of bloodlust.

Their affair lasted as long as Aphrodite's marriage to her real husband, Hephaestus. In turn, their forbidden union gave birth to numerous offspring such as Eros, Deimos, Phobos and Enteros. These children, bearing the lineage of the goddess of love, ruled over various emotions and states of mind. Eros governed over the process of falling in love. He is also better known as Cupid.

Despite the secrecy between the two, Helios the sun god had spied on Ares and Aphrodite laying together and reported their adultery to Hephaestus, known as the smith god who created Zeus' thunderbolts.

In anger, Hephaestus created a chain that could not be broken and laid it along his bed in an attempt to catch the adulterous lovers in action. Hephaestus then travelled to his patron city to catch Ares in the act of committing adultery once again with his wife. Ares, seizing the opportunity, called unto Aphrodite to make love to her once more. There, the chains sprung forth and bound them together.

In this state, Hephaestus called forth all the deities of Olympus to show them his discover. This brought about the divorce between Hephaestus and Aphrodite. Claiming his prize, Hephaestus ordered that the chains shall not be removed unless Zeus returned all the betrothal he initially gave him in pursuit of Aphrodite.

"She has beauty but no sense of shame." Were his words as described by poets. Following the incident, Aphrodite and Ares were then freed from their shackles and Hephaestus was cleared of his duties as husband to her. In stories that followed this scene, Hephaestus was depicted having another wife while Ares and Aphrodite were free to consummate their feelings for each other.

Besides affairs with other gods, Aphrodite was also known to have had relationships with mortals whom she fancied. Most popular of these unions was her affair with a mortal named Adonis. She would watch him hunt in the forest from a distance making sure that he was safe from harm as he hunted with his dogs.

This affection did not please Ares, who sent a wild boar to kill the man during one of his hunting trips. Aphrodite doted over the corpse of Adonis, which caused red roses to form for every drop of blood that fell from his body.

Upon reaching the underworld, Persephone, the wife of Hades, also took a liking to the very handsome Adonis. Almost every creature in the mortal world mourned for his death, which moved Hades and Zeus. Given the situation, Zeus decreed that Adonis should spend four months with Aphrodite and another four months in the underworld with Persephone. He was free to do as he pleased with the rest of the year.

Another notable tale surrounding Aphrodite was her involvement in one of the greatest wars fought in Greek history, the Trojan War.

In a competition to see who was the fairest in the land, Zeus decreed a contest during a banquet to have a mere mortal decide who wins the title. The mortal was the Trojan prince Paris, who was deeply enamored with Helen, the wife of the King of Sparta.

In an attempt to win the competition, Aphrodite promised Paris that Helen would fall in love with him if he declared Aphrodite to be the most beautiful being in all of Greece. Tantalized by this promise, Paris chose Aphrodite and the goddess fulfilled her end of the bargain.

When Helen and Paris absconded for Troy, her husband, King Menelaus, set out after her, calling his allies to arms for assistance. This uprising led to the Trojan War and the epics of other heroes such as Hector and Achilles.

Apollo

The favored god of bards and poets, Apollo governed most of the arts such as music and poetry. He was also known as the god of archery and disease. His symbols included a bow and arrow and of course, the lyre.

Born of the union between Zeus and Leto, Apollo was unique in the sense that his birth was from the pairing of a Titan and an Olympian. He was born alongside his twin, the goddess Artemis, on the island of Delos. Their birth was another legend inscribed and romanticized in tales by the poets.

Despising the union of Zeus and Leto, Hera sent forth monsters and mortals to hunt Leto who was pregnant with the twin gods at the time. She was not given a chance to rest nor give birth safely due to this. It was on the island of Delos that she found refuge and was finally able to give birth to the twins.

This gave the floating island a special importance to the twins and Leto, which became a place for their mother to rest. One time, when she was visiting the island, a giant named Tityus attempted to abduct Leto, alarming her children. In an attempt to save his mother, Apollo drew out his bow and quiver and showered the giant with arrows, slaying the creature and saving his mother.

Apollo is also known to represent the energy and fondness of youth, because he was very close to younger Greeks. This fondness was best reflected in the myth of how he created the flower known as Hyacinth.

This name first belonged to a young Greek boy Hyacinthus. Such was the boy's beauty that it attracted Apollo and inspired a relationship between the two. During their time together, they used Discus throwing as entertainment.

On one such occasion, Apollo threw the discus and Hyacinthus ran to catch it in an attempt to impress the god. It was then that the jealous god of the North Wind intervened and caused the discus to veer off-track. This event caused the discus to strike Hyacinthus in the head, killing him instantly.

Many paintings depict his death, with Apollo doting over the corpse. Saddened by the loss of his lover, Apollo struck a deal with Hades who was to take the boy to the underworld. Instead of taking him, Apollo turned the boy into a flower which became known as the Hyacinth. He created the flower from his blood and stained its petals with his tears.

Another story of note was Apollo's duel with a satyr by the name of Marsyas. He was known to have found the flute created by Athena, who didn't like how the instrument was played. Confident in his skills, he challenged Apollo to a musical contest. Being unfamiliar with the instrument and its charms, Apollo lost to the satyr in the first round of their bout.

Unwilling to yield, Apollo demanded that the second round entail them playing their instruments upside-down. Provided that the flute could only be played one way, the satyr lost and was punished by the angry Apollo. He was tied to a tree as his skin was peeled off him alive.

Ares

Popularly known as the god of war, Ares was recognized as the harbinger of bloodlust. This made him quite famous among soldiers and mercenaries who wanted to make a name for themselves. Being the god of war, he was symbolized by weapons and armor. He was also often depicted in art as wearing a helmet or holding one to his side.

Of all the stories and myths about Ares, it is interesting to see that his most famous tale was that of romance instead of war. It was well-known throughout Olympus that he was affectionate towards the goddess of love, Aphrodite, and that she shared his affection for the fearsome god of war.

Unfortunately, Zeus used Aphrodite as a bargaining chip with the smith lord Hephaestus in order to convince him to free Hera from imprisonment. The smith god agreed and offered betrothal gifts to the lord of Olympus in order to claim the goddess of love as his wife.

Having been claimed by someone other than himself, Ares resorted to adultery to continue his relationship with Aphrodite. This did not end well for the both of them for Helios discovered their affair and reported it to her husband.

Naturally, Areas also had a history of being a vengeful god. Many tales speak about his wrath for injustices being done to him and his children.

Most notable of these tales of retribution was his murder of Halirrhothius, the son of Poseidon. It was said that the man fell in love and desired Ares' daughter Alkippe. This led him to rape the girl and incite the rage of the god of war. In anger, Ares killed Halirrhothius and was put on trial for this act of revenge.

Ares was also known for punishing those who went against him and his creations. One popular myth was his revenge on King Cadmus, who had slain Ares' serpent that was guarding a magical spring. Cadmus needed to draw water from it for a certain ritual, but was met with the god's wrath instead.

What's interesting here is that Ares' retribution did not come instantly. The god of bloodlust waited for the perfect time to strike. It was during a time of weakness that Ares turned the king into a snake, befitting his incursion against the god of war.

Sadly, his wife, Harmonia, who was Ares' daughter with Athena, mourned the fate of her husband and cried to the gods that she be turned into one as well. Feeling no remorse, Ares gave in to her request and allowed the couple to live as serpents.

Interestingly, Ares also meddled in the Trojan War, but not of his accord. At the start of the conflict, Ares claimed indifference to the outcome of the war. However, he was convinced by his lover,

Aphrodite to support the Trojans. This might have been because of the goddess' involvement in the war as well.

Despite his participation, Ares was wounded by a spear during the war and headed back to Olympus in order to heal himself. Aphrodite also did not escape injury during this upheaval.

It is said that the fury of Ares did not manifest itself in individual acts of retribution, but rallied themselves in the form of wars. People would usually attribute great wars and conflicts as events that happen under the will of Ares.

Artemis

Known as the goddess of the hunt, she was also the twin sister of Apollo and they shared the bow and arrow as a symbol. They were considered to be guardians of the youth; with Apollo watching over boys and Artemis watching over girls.

It was said that Artemis was the older of the twins, coming out of her mother Leto before her twin brother. She served as a midwife for her mother as she finally gave birth to Apollo.

One notable story for Artemis was her creation of the constellation Orion. Before he became the constellation of stars we know today, Orion was a handsome giant that won the favor of the goddess of the hunt. Artemis would occasionally require his companionship during hunting sessions where he would serve the goddess well.

It was during one hunt, that his servitude finally. Orion claimed that he was master of the wilderness as he guarded Artemis. He claimed that there was no beast that he would not be able to deal with quickly.

This statement angered the gods and caused Gaia of the Earth to create a scorpion with which to harm Artemis. In an effort to protect the goddess, Orion blocked the scorpion and took the sting for her instead. This led to his demise at due to a beast of the earth, a contradiction to his claim.

Saddened by this loss, Artemis pleaded with Zeus who was also moved by the service Orion had given to his daughter. Instead of being banished into the underworld, Zeus turned Orion into a constellation which decorated the sky at night.

Interestingly, the scorpion that led to his death was also turned into a constellation. We know it today as the constellation of Scorpio.

Artemis was also known to be cunning and wise. This was seen most during her defense of Olympus from the attack of the Aloadai giants. These were the sons of Poseidon with a titan. When Otos and Ephialtes came of age, they decided to challenge the gods for a chance to live in Olympus. They wished to claim Hera and Artemis as their brides.

In one cunning move, Artemis turned herself into a deer and led the two giants into a chase. She then darted in between them as they were about to skewer her with their lances. But with her skill and speed, both giants missed and wounded each other in the process instead.

Much like her brother, Artemis was also known to be vengeful. This is all because of her punishment directed at Actaeon.

It was during a hunt that Artemis decided to bathe in one of the small lakes in Gargaphia. There, she was spied upon by another hunter, Actaeon, who was looking for a place in which he can rest with his many hunting hounds. Artemis caught the hunter spying on her as she bathed, and was so enraged by the breach of privacy that her revenge came swiftly.

She turned him into a stag so that he couldn't talk. Unfortunately, in this form, his own hunting hounds could no longer discern the image of their master and as such, they attacked and mauled him to death.

Artemis was also involved in the creation of another constellation, Ursa Major, also known as the giant bear.

It was through an affair between Zeus and a nymph Callisto that this story came to pass. Callisto was a forest nymph and a daughter of king Lycaon of Arcadia. The nymph daughter of the King attracted the lord of Olympus who then seduced her.

Naturally, Hera had gotten wind of this affair and punished the nymph by turning her into a bear, destined to roam the woods. Artemis, during one of her hunts, ends up killing the nymph in bear form—not knowing who it was at first. Upon recognizing who the bear was originally, Artemis made her a constellation instead of sending her to live in the underworld.

Athena

Athena is historically known as the goddess of wisdom, sound judgment, and of war. She was a favorite among those who needed advice amidst personal confusion. It must be noted that she does not share this title with Ares. Ares was the god of bloodlust driven from war while Athena governed the art of war itself.

Unlike other gods who were born from mothers who slept with a god or a titan, the story behind the birth of Athena was a little similar to the creation of Aphrodite.

Allegedly the daughter of Metis, Athena was born from inside Zeus, her father. When Zeus learned that Metis was pregnant, he was warned by Gaia that this offspring would rise to overthrow him just as he did to his own father.

Fearing the end of his reign, Zeus swallowed Metis without even waiting for her to give birth. This led to Zeus experiencing terrible headaches and stomach pain. He confided in Hephaestus about these pains, but couldn't do much about it. In an effort to relieve his pain, Hephaestus cleaved Zeus' forehead and from there, Athena sprung, already fully equipped in armor.

One important story of Athena was how she became the patron goddess of the city of Athens. Stories would speak of a rivalry between her and Zeus' brother, Poseidon. Both deities wanted to become the favored god of the famous city, so they held a competition to see who was the most deserving of it.

Athena began by using her powers to summon an olive tree upon the citadel of Athens. Poseidon on the other hand, wanted to give better offering to the city by causing a spring to flow up from the same place. Unfortunately, the water that came from the spring was salty and of little use to the citizens. This made the olive tree a more useful gift and earned Athena the favor of the Athenians.

Athena was also known to interfere with the quests of many heroes. She helped Perseus behead the Medusa by advising him not to look at the monster in the eye. Some poets say she lent the demigod a helping hand out of her desire to have the head of Medusa decorate her shield.

Athena also helped Hercules with the first of his twelve tasks; the Nemean Lion. Although she did not help the hero slay the beast, it was with the subsequent problem that she proved most useful. Having a very thick mane and skin, Hercules was having difficulty skinning the lion for its mane. If he was unable to do this, his efforts to slay the lion would not be recognized and it would have been deemed as a failure despite him being able to kill the animal.

Disguised as an old woman, Athena came to Hercules in that dark hour and advised him to look to the claws of the lion for help. Since the lion had great claws, it was only logical that these weapons would be the only tool that could handle its own skin. With that in mind, Hercules was able to complete his first task and come back triumphantly.

She also helped Jason and the Argonauts by watching over them as they built their ship, enchanting the wood that was being used as the ship's mast. There are other tales in countless other adventures of different heroes that speak of Athena's guidance and help, allowing the protagonists to conquer their adversaries.

Demeter

Demeter was recognized as the patron goddess of the fields. She was the goddess favored by the farmers and harvesters that regularly depended on her grace. Being the goddess of agriculture, she was usually depicted with stems of wheat and a torch.

The most interesting story of Demeter was the rape of her daughter Persephone, by the god of the underworld, Hades. Zeus had helped his brother Hades kidnap Demeter's daughter, which then caused the goddess to roam the lands in search of her daughter. It was during this time that she caught the eye of Zeus' other brother, Poseidon.

She was known to have become a love interest of the god of the sea, Poseidon. After lusting for her, Poseidon followed Demeter on her quest to find her daughter. Aware of the wiles of the sea god, Demeter turned herself into a mare and hid herself amongst the other horses at a watering hole.

Poseidon, learning of this act of cunning, turned himself into a stallion and claimed Demeter as a horse. This, of course, angered the goddess of the fields but she managed to set aside her anger and instead chose to bathe herself in the same river.

When she had learned of the whereabouts of her daughter, she travelled to Eleusis to plan her revenge. It was then that she was invited to sit with the women surrounding the King of Eleusis, who were able to make laugh and smile. This, in some way, appeased her anger.

Most notable of Demeter's contributions to society was the sending of the hero Triptolemos to teach agriculture to the earth.

Being an Eleusinian prince, he accepted Demeter into his house during the time the goddess was grieving over the loss of her daughter Persephone to Hades. Upon resolution of the conflict and the return of Persephone to her mother, Demeter decided to impart the gift of agriculture to mankind.

She sought out the prince and gave him the knowledge to till the lands and reap the gifts the earth has to offer. She also gave the prince a chariot that had wings and was pulled by serpents. This was meant to enable Triptolemos to go around the world, teaching the people the benefits of agriculture.

Dionysus

Being the god of wine, merry-making and revelry, he was a favorite among nobles and elites who loved to throw feasts and sleep with multiple partners. Dionysus was the son of Zeus who fathered him with a mortal named Semele. She was the princess of Thebes during the time of his inception.

Dionysus was carried by his father Zeus until his birth. During the pregnancy of Semele, Hera tricked her into demanding that Zeus show himself to her in all his glory.

When Zeus followed suit, Semele was killed by the searing heat of his thunderbolts that decorated the god's real form. Distraught by the sad turn of events, Zeus took his unborn son and carried him within his thigh to help him grow and be born as a god.

In his youth, it was Dionysus who discovered the joy of wine and the secret of the grapevine. It was during his time with the nymphs of Nysa that he learned how to make wine from grapes that grew from vines.

Among his many notable feats would be conquering India with one of the most unique armies ever assembled. With a plethora of satyrs, demigods and other beings, he began his expedition to India and left his Theban kingdom under the care of his trusted nurse, Nysus.

After conquering India and establishing his worshippers there, he returned to a steward who was unwilling to hand back his kingdom. This led to his attempt to reclaim the kingdom by using his own cunning and using a feast in order to disguise his real intent.

After having waited for three years, Dionysus asked Nysus to allow him to perform a ritual at a ceremony within the Theban Kingdom as he usually would. There, he disguised his soldiers in women's clothing to get them inside the kingdom. Once inside, the battle for ownership ensued and Dionysus was able to eventually reclaim his kingdom.

Hephaestus

Recognized as the god of fire, Hephaestus was also deemed as the patron god of stonemasonry, smithing and sculpture, making him a favorite among various artisans. He was known to have created a great many artifacts during his time which were of great use to many gods and heroes.

The most noticeable thing about the smith god was the fact that he limped, unlike the other gods who were born a close to perfection as possible. Many sources attribute this to the idea that he was born from Hera without uniting with Zeus.

Being born in such a state, he was cast out of Olympus. He continued to fall from the heavens for one whole day before finally falling into the ocean. Fortunately, two sea-goddesses came to his aide and allowed him to dwell with them in their underwater grotto.

From there, he started a small forge in which he created some of the most exquisite jewelry as payment to the goddesses that took him in, despite him being lame and unable to walk properly. The goddesses Thetis and Eurynome were greatly pleased with these trinkets and wore them wherever they went.

It was during an audience with Hera that these trinkets caught the eye of the gods. The wife of Zeus took notice of these accessories and asked the both sea-goddesses where they got them. Naturally, it came to Hera that it was her outcast son, Hephaestus, who forged them. Suddenly seeing the value in her offspring, she made him come back to Olympus where she gave him an even bigger forge.

One of the most notable stories surrounding Hephaestus was the creation of Pandora and her box.

At the beginning of times, Zeus instructed Hephaestus to mold a model for the first woman on earth; that woman became Pandora. She was a beautiful being who won the favor of Zeus, who originally meant for the woman to be a punishment to the brothers Epimetheus and Prometheus, who gave mankind the underserving gift of fire.

Having created Pandora from mere clay, Hephaestus did such an impressive job that even Hera was pleased and breathed life into the piece. After that, the other gods blessed Pandora with other desirable qualities such as beauty and intellect. Hermes also gifted the woman with cunning and deceit. When she was ready, she was sent to earth as a form of present.

Epimetheus was instantly taken by Pandora and decided to marry her. As a gift, Zeus gave Pandora a beautiful box. He instructed Pandora to never open the box. However, Pandora's natural curiosity got the best of her and she decided to open the box when her husband was not looking.

From the box came disease and chaos which began to plague mankind. Lastly, there came hope—the final thing that the box released unto the world.

Hera

Whenever Zeus had an affair, Hera would always be in the picture. Having been chosen as the official wife of Zeus, she had made it her duty to watch over her husbands' indiscretions and punish the women who seduced the king of Olympus.

Considered as the queen of the gods, she presided as the goddess of marriage and the night sky. Artists would usually paint her as a beautiful woman with a scepter.

One famous story concerning Hera was how Zeus seduced her. Being infatuated with the young goddess, Zeus turned himself into a cuckoo bird in order to win her favor. Hera, being fond of the bird, took a liking to it and claimed it as her own pet.

It was later on that Zeus claimed Hera as his bride. It was a grand wedding in which all the gods participated. Their union brought Ares and Hebe to the Olympians. Sadly, this wedding was the last romantic gesture between the two, for Zeus had started wooing other women right after marrying Hera.

Hera was known to be a very jealous wife, a fact which is depicted in many stories, showing how cruel her punishments can be for both men and women who displeased her. One of the most notable stories was what she did to Hercules.

Being the son of Zeus with another woman and having been gifted with incredible strength, Hera swelled with jealousy. This caused her to make the child's life difficult from the beginning, but the most notable act of spite took place during Hercules' adulthood.

Married to Megara, the princess of Thebes, Hercules had five children. He started a happy family with his wife; a fact that did not please the queen of the gods. One night, Hera tampered with Hercules' mind, driving him crazy.

In his fit of madness, he was led to believe that he was engaged in combat with his enemies when in truth, he was assaulting his own family. When he came to his senses, he was left with the sight of his victims. They also began to haunt him in his dreams.

Drowning in remorse and needing forgiveness, Hercules consulted Apollo and was advised to serve under King Eurystheus of Mycenae. Here, Hera made her move once again by convincing the king to give Hercules the most difficult of tasks. This is where the 12 epic labor of Hercules began.

Besides Hercules, Hera also showed her displeasure to countless other mortals that crossed paths with her husband. She was the one who assaulted Leto, the mother of Apollo and Artemis and forced her to give secretly birth on a faraway island.

On the other hand, Hera also had her share of encounters with men, such as the incident with Ixion who attempted to rape her. Upon reporting this to Zeus, the god first gave the suspect a test to make sure that his wife was speaking the truth.

Fashioning an image of Hera from a cloud, he placed it beside Ixion during slumber and waited for the mortal's reaction. Come morning, Ixion bragged about his exploit with the queen of the gods, thus confirming Hera's story. As punishment Zeus attached the mortal to a flaming wheel which hung from the skies.

Despite the mostly negative image of Hera as a jealous and scornful wife, she also had her share of favors with certain individuals. One of them was with the hero Jason who benefitted from Hera's aide during his quest for the Golden Fleece.

Hermes

Known as the god of cunning and thievery, his mischief was legendary among mortals and immortals alike. Given his dominion over such qualities, it was natural for him to be coy and charming, able to manipulate people and gods into doing his will.

Hermes was the son of Zeus to a nymph named Maia. In order to escape the wrath of a jealous Hera, Maia gave birth inside a cave.

Upon birth, Hermes was already capable of great mischief. One of his earliest pranks included creating a lyre from the shell of a turtle and stealing cattle from the god Apollo. These antics won him the favor of his father who, in turn, offered him a seat as one of the 12 gods of Olympus.

Hermes also played vital roles in epic missions such as helping Perseus on his quest by allowing him to use his winged sandals and giving him the power to fly without the help of Pegasus. He also lent the hero the helmet of Hades which allowed the wearer to become invisible. Upon completion of his quest, Perseus returned these items to Hermes.

He also played part in the creation of the giant Orion, as promised to King Hyrieus of Thrace. The King had asked for children after he gave Poseidon, Zeus and Hermes a warm welcome to his kingdom. The three gods urinated on the hide of a sacrificial bull used for their visit. From this act, the giant Orion was born.

He was also known to have helped Hercules complete one of his most dangerous tasks, fetching one of the hounds who were under Hades' care. For this, Hermes acted as a guide while the hero treaded through the world of the undead in order to complete his task.

As a messenger of the gods, Hermes is often seen in various stories, carrying out wills and helping people to whom the gods have shown favor. He was known to provide knowledge and tools that would help heroes complete their missions.

But he wasn't just a messenger. He was also known for defeating the giant Hippolytus with his golden sword during the war of the giants at Olympus. He was also there when Zeus was defeated by the giant Typhoeus, helping his father regain his strength to finally win against the oppressor.

It was also Hermes that gifted Pandora with deceit and playfulness, two characteristics that endeared her to Epimetheus. In order for Zeus' punishment to be dealt properly, Pandora needed to capture the hearts of either one of the brothers. Hermes' gifts to the girl allowed her to accomplish exactly that.

Interestingly, Hermes also had an affair with the goddess of love, Aphrodite. Their union gave birth to Hermaphroditus. His was an interesting story that sprung from the love of a nymph named Salmacis. Having fallen madly in love with the beautiful son of Hermes, the nymph wished for her to never be parted from him. Olympus answered her prayers and permanently made her part of the boy. This is where the term Hermaphrodite comes from, a word which means having both male and female genitalia.

The Most Powerful Gods

Of all the ancient Greek gods, there were three that reigned over all of them in terms of power and governance. Although Zeus was deemed almighty, he had two brothers which he shared dominion over the rest of the earth. Just like Zeus, they had their own share of romances and adventures that added more color to Greek mythology.

Poseidon

Hailed as god of the sea, he ruled with over bodies of water, floods, earthquakes, and horses. He was often depicted riding a chariot that's being pulled by majestic sea-horses.

Poseidon was one of the children of Chronos, and among those whom the titan had eaten in attempts to quell the threat of rebellion from his children. He was rescued by Zeus with the help of Metis who brought about the death of Chronos.

During the Titanomachy, the giants helped Poseidon by fashioning a mighty trident for the god of the sea. Using this gift, Poseidon defeated the elder titans along with his brothers and sent them to the black pits of Tartaros. With that gift, Poseidon continued ruling over the seas, his area of dominion.

Just like his brother Zeus, Poseidon was wily and had a habit of running after objects or women that had taken his fancy despite him being married to Amphrite. One of the most notable romantic conquests of Poseidon was that of the maiden Medusa.

Before she turned into a monster, Medusa was a very beautiful maiden who served in the temple of Athena. There, she was seduced by Poseidon and he claimed her within the very walls of the temple.

The goddess Athena thought of this as an act of blasphemy and cast a curse upon the beautiful woman.

She was turned into a monster. Her long hair turned into a bouquet of poisonous snakes and her stare was made to turn any man into stone. She then played part in the epic of Perseus who ended up beheading her and using her head to slay another one of Poseidon's children; the Kraken.

Besides Medusa, Poseidon had a long list of other lovers with whom he had different offspring. He was also known to have fathered the flying horse known as Pegasus, who was born from his very union with Medusa. It is quite an ironic turn of events to see that his other son, Perseus, would receive his own half-brother in the form of an animal as a gift in order to safely travel to the chambers of his father's lover.

Another notable contribution given by Poseidon is the beast called the Minotaur. This creature was a combination man and bull who also became the guardian of the labyrinth at Knossos. Poseidon was offended by King Minos of Knossos sacrificing a bull in his name. This act caused Poseidon to place Minos' wife in a trance and have her make love to a bull. This unlikely union brought forth the beast which was then locked away in a labyrinth out of shame.

One notable thing about Poseidon was the fact that he did not reside on mount Olympus like the other gods despite being one of the most powerful one. He decided to watch over his domain within the sea itself, along with his wife. It was only during important gatherings at Olympus that Poseidon would grace the mountain with his presence.

Another legendary story about Poseidon was his participation in the founding of Troy. This task came as a punishment for his attempt to overthrow Zeus from Olympus, alongside Athena. His efforts to create the walls of Troy were spoken of in high regard during the Trojan War. The walls were deemed unbreakable until Achilles decided to use cunning and treachery, making use of the wooden horse to get soldiers through the gates.

Hades

Recognized as the god of the underworld, Hades was the often seen as then unfortunate god who drew the worst of the lot, ending up with the land of the dead to govern over. This is despite him being the eldest among the three brothers. He would be depicted by most artists as a bearded man who was always accompanied by his underworld servant, Cerberus. A three-headed dog that guarded the gates of the underworld.

Like Poseidon, Hades did not reside on mount Olympus despite his prominence. Instead, he lived within the underworld to watch over the souls that get ferried over into the afterlife.

Interestingly, Hades was not depicted as evil, unlike many modern popular art and culture interpretations of him. Instead, he was depicted as a straightforward god that paid little attention to what went on in the world of mortals. As far as he was concerned, his main focus was to ensure that none of his subjects who came to serve him in the underworld ever went back to the world of the living.

However, just like his brothers, Hades also felt the need of female company. With the help of his brother Zeus, he staged the kidnapping of one of Demeter's daughters' Persephone, to whom he had taken a liking to.

As Persephone was out in the fields picking flowers, she came upon an enchanted narcissus among the plants. Curious and charmed, the maiden plucked the flower. Little did she know that this was a trap set by Hades to kidnap her and make her his bride. As soon as she took the flower, the ground opened up and Hades appeared on his chariot and horses to take her to the underworld.

What happened after was a threat from Persephone's mother Demeter that she will abdicate her duties as the goddess of the fertile earth if her daughter was not returned to her.

In order to keep Persephone to himself, Hades fed her the seeds of a Pomegranate which was designed to magically bind anyone who ate it to the underworld. But with Demeter's demands, Zeus was left with no choice but to decree that Persephone spend half of the year with her husband Hades and the other half in the living world with her mother.

Zeus

Heralded as the mightiest of the gods, it was Zeus who brought about the rule of his generation during the Titanomachy. He was the hand that dealt the finishing blow to Chronus which allowed him to demand the release of his siblings from the belly of the titan.

Zeus was spared from the fate of his siblings with the help of his mother. He was spirited away and was raised far from Chronos—who still believed that the rock he swallowed was his child, Zeus.

He was raised and nursed by the nymphs and was guarded over by the warrior Curetes. In the island he was sent to, he continued to live in peace until he came of age. It is then that he began plotting to regain control over the heavens and defeat the titans.

With the help of the goddess Metis, Zeus was able to coax Chronus to regurgitate his siblings who then came to his aide during the Titanomachy. On top of that, Zeus also worked to free the giants from Tartaros, who gifted him with the iconic thunderbolts he used to win the war along with his brothers Poseidon and Hades.

Having been granted dominion over the sky, Zeus ruled the heavens from his throne on mount Olympus. Despite only having one-third of the world to rule, he had the final say in most things. He was called in to settle disputes between gods and meted out punishment to those who committed treason and other forms of treachery on Olympus.

Despite most songs speaking of his infidelity, he was a just ruler. He favored those who prioritized justice and charity. He was also severe on those who preyed on the weak. This is also the reason why he showed favor to his sons such as Hercules and Hermes.

With his mistresses, Zeus fathered many beings, both divine and mortal. Most of his mortal offspring became kings or important people around the world such as King Minos and Helen of Troy.

47680131R00045

Made in the USA
Middletown, DE
31 August 2017